Publishing Credits

Dona Herweck Rice, *Editor-in-Chief*
Lee Aucoin, *Creative Director*
Kristy Stark, M.A.Ed., *Senior Editor*
Torrey Maloof, *Editor*
Kristine Magnien, M.S.Ed., *Associate Education Editor*
Neri Garcia, *Senior Designer*
Stephanie Reid, *Photo Researcher*
Rachelle Cracchiolo, M.S.Ed., *Publisher*

Image Credits

cover: Thinkstock; pp. 3, 9, 12, 40 iStockphoto; all other images Shutterstock.

Teacher Created Materials

5301 Oceanus Drive
Huntington Beach, CA 92649-1030
http://www.tcmpub.com
ISBN 978-1-4333-5269-0
© 2013 Teacher Created Materials, Inc.
Printed in China
WaiMan.012021

Table of Contents

Dear Family,

Welcome to fourth grade! This is an important transition year for your child. In fourth grade, students are expected to read more challenging textbooks. You'll no doubt be hearing more about history and science as your child begins doing some research projects as well. Oh, and you'll probably be brushing up on those long division skills very soon, too!

Your child's after-school interests may become more demanding. Things like sports, music, and organized groups all take time. Your child may want to have more time for friends, perhaps wanting to do school projects together. This is a great year to begin releasing more responsibility to your child, like taking the lead for his or her school requirements. This parent guide will give you some tips for starting that transition, too.

Take a bit of time to find out how your child's teacher prefers to communicate with families. You'll want to stay in touch and build a partnership so that the year will go smoothly. It will pay off on those busy days when other demands (e.g., errands, jobs, other children) keep you on the run.

One last thought...

Your child may seem old enough to be more independent. But, he or she still needs adults—parents, grandparents, or other caretakers—who ensure that fourth grade is a year of learning and fun!

Getting
a Good Start

Capitalize on those school expectations of your child taking on more responsibility. Teachers expect that students at this age will be increasingly self-sufficient. You should expect the same at home.

These ideas will help everyone begin and end the day more smoothly.

Time Management

Good habits aren't built overnight. If your child struggles with time management, be ready to step in and monitor after-school activities.

Checklists

Post checklists and reminders to help your child establish consistent routines and habits.

In- and Out-Boxes

Have your child empty his or her backpack after school and place homework and papers that need to be reviewed in the in-box. Once the work is complete, move it to the out-box.

Pack It Up

Collect the papers from the out-box and have your child put them in his or her backpack the night before. This way, he or she is ready for the morning rush.

SCHEDULE

4:00	Snack
4:30	Piano practice
5:00	Set the table, feed the dog
5:30	Dinner
6:30	Homework and reading time
7:00	Free time (after homework)
7:30	Get ready for bed

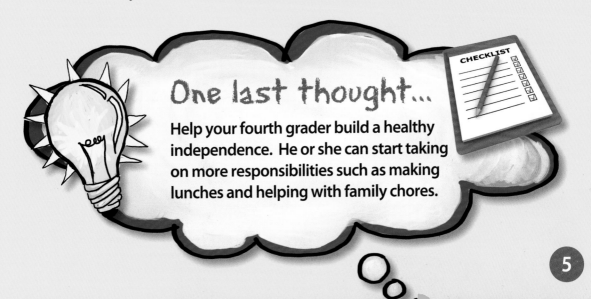

One last thought...

Help your fourth grader build a healthy independence. He or she can start taking on more responsibilities such as making lunches and helping with family chores.

CHECKLIST

Homework
Helpers

Your fourth grader may be expected to do 40 or more minutes of homework each night. Managing time will become more and more important for your child.

Review

Begin by reviewing assignments. Start with the toughest assignments first. Decide what needs to be done to meet due dates on longer projects. This will keep everyone from going into panic mode later.

Small Steps

Your child needs manageable steps. Be the "guide on the side," helping your child make steady progress without becoming frustrated. Have plenty of supplies on hand.

One last thought...

Be patient—talk through the problem, but don't do the work for your child.

$8\overline{)40}$

Keep Talking

Your fourth grader may be less willing to talk about the school day. One-word answers are common to questions such as: What did you do in school today? (Nothing.) How was school? (Fine.) Do you have homework? (No.) This is the time to develop some good communication skills and keep the conversations going.

Try these ideas to get your child talking.

What would you have done differently today if you were the teacher?

What was the most interesting thing you learned today? Why?

What was your favorite subject today? Why?

One last thought...

Open communication is crucial as your child gets older. Your fourth grader may face situations, such as bullying, that you'll want to discuss more fully. If anything comes up that is troubling, be sure to contact your child's teacher.

Sleep Your
Way Smart

Fourth graders are facing more pressure this year, so getting a good night's sleep is increasingly important. Now, I'm sure you've heard, "But I'm not tired!" However, you need to ensure that your fourth grader is well rested.

Here are some tips for making sure your fourth grader gets enough sleep.

Early Bird Dinner

Have dinner at least two hours before bed. Avoid caffeine or sugary snacks.

You Snooze, You Lose

Don't let your child sleep "just a few more minutes" in the morning. It's the routine that matters!

The chart below shows how much sleep children need.

Age	Sleep Needed
1–3 years	12–14 hours
3–5 years	11–13 hours
5–12 years	10–11 hours

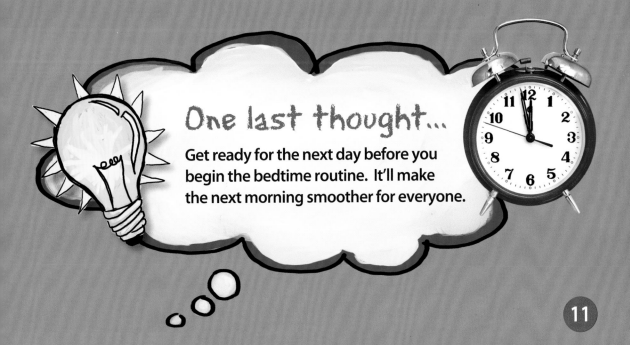

One last thought...

Get ready for the next day before you begin the bedtime routine. It'll make the next morning smoother for everyone.

Top 10 Things
Your Fourth Grader
Needs to Know

1. **Write a paragraph** (a topic sentence, three supporting details, and a closing sentence)

2. **Complex cause-and-effect** relationships

3. **Strategies to draw meaning** from stories

4. **Decimals and fractions** (add, subtract, and compare)

5. **Multiply multi-digit numbers** by two-digit numbers

6. **Divide multi-digit numbers** by one-digit numbers (long division)

7. **Overview of life, earth, and physical sciences** (e.g., comparing animals, introduction to weather, and sources of light and energy)

8. **Ask questions about objects and organisms** and use data to make a reasonable explanation

9. Your **state's history**

10. **American Indian tribes** that lived in your state

Words

on the Go

Fourth graders are expanding their vocabulary as they read a variety of different texts. Having strong vocabulary skills pays off as they encounter new words!

These word games will help your fourth grader build his or her vocabulary.

Homophones

A homophone is a word that is pronounced the same as another word, but has a different meaning. When you notice homophones in the world around you, try pointing them out. "The word *brake* has two meanings in that sign. What is the other meaning and spelling?"

Anagrams

Anagrams are made by rearranging the letters in one word to make a new word. "Look at the word *meat*. Can you figure out three more words you can make with those letters?" (*team, mate, and tame*)

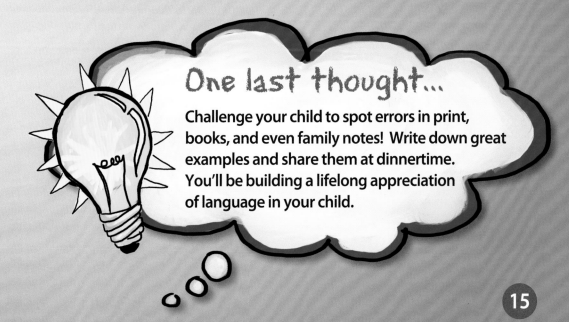

One last thought...

Challenge your child to spot errors in print, books, and even family notes! Write down great examples and share them at dinnertime. You'll be building a lifelong appreciation of language in your child.

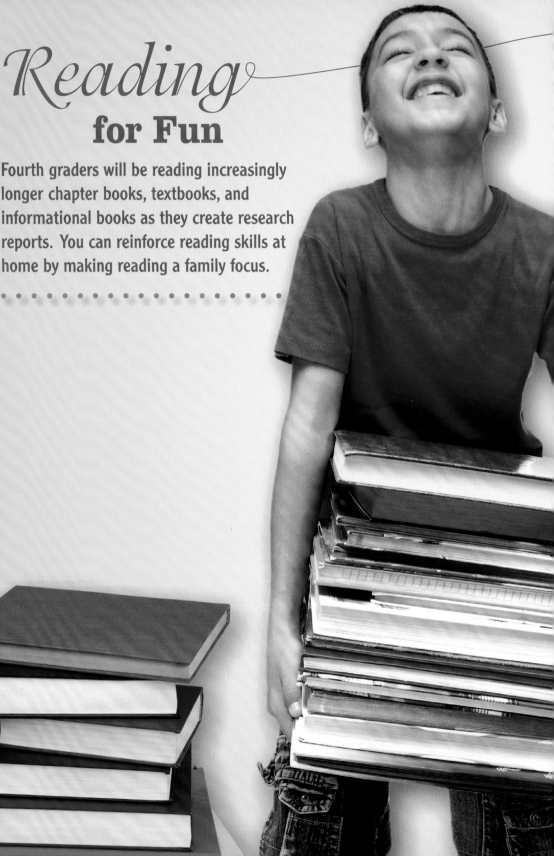

Reading
for Fun

Fourth graders will be reading increasingly longer chapter books, textbooks, and informational books as they create research reports. You can reinforce reading skills at home by making reading a family focus.

These activities will help improve your child's reading skills.

Book Project

Have your child create a project that represents the book he or she is reading. Crossword puzzles, cartoon strips, collages, murals, time lines, and dioramas are all great ideas.

Book Award

Create a family award for the best book of the week, month, or year. Read a series by a single author, then give an award for the best of the series. Keep a journal that captures the ratings and best (and worst) features of the books.

Magazines

Subscribe to a content-area magazine such as *Dig* (archaeology), *Faces* (people around the world), or *Muse* (history, science, and the arts) for your child.

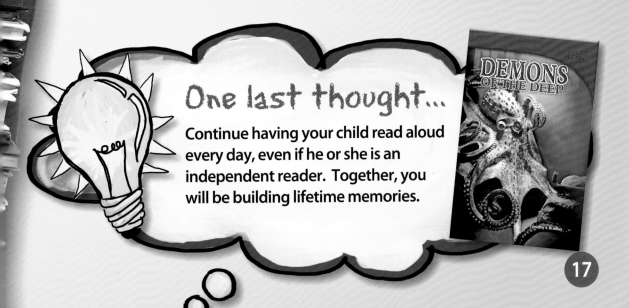

One last thought...

Continue having your child read aloud every day, even if he or she is an independent reader. Together, you will be building lifetime memories.

DEMONS OF THE DEEP

Timothy J. Bradley

Building
a Library

Your child's library speaks volumes about his and her likes and dislikes. This is the time to organize and expand the library, filling it with useful reference books, additional series books, and informational books.

Here are some tips for how to find books.

- **Sales at bookstores**
- **Book swap with neighbors**
- **Library book sales**
- **Garage sales**

Here are some books your fourth grader may enjoy.

Bud, Not Buddy by Christopher Paul Curtis

Tales of a Fourth Grade Nothing by Judy Blume

Hoot by Carl Hiaasen

Dear Mr. Henshaw by Beverly Cleary

Peter and the Starcatchers
by Dave Barry and Ridley Pearson

James and the Giant Peach by Roald Dahl

Wayside School by Louis Sachar

Maniac McGee by Jerry Spinelli

Frindle by Andrew Clements

Diary of a Wimpy Kid by Jeff Kinney

One last thought...

Take time to read some of the chapter books that your youngster is reading. You'll discover that there are some terrific books available, no matter what age they say on the cover!

Writing
and Spelling

As your fourth grader gains more experiences with writing, spelling will become more important. Practice those really difficult words called spelling demons, such as *early*, *heard*, *high*, and *weigh*. Also, watch for those words with similar spellings such as *dairy* and *diary* or *where*, *we're*, *wear*, and *were*.

Make preparing for spelling tests more fun with some of these strategies.

To make most words plural, add *s*: *dog, dogs*

If a word ends in *y*, drop the *y* and add *ies*: *pony, ponies*

If a word ends in *s*, *ch*, *sh*, or *x*, add *es*: *kiss, kisses; punch, punches; dish, dishes; box, boxes*

If a word ends in *f*, change the *f* to *ves*: *leaf, leaves* (Except for words like *chef*. Then just add the s.)

The Write Coach

Prewriting
This is the brainstorming stage when key ideas or words can be discussed and jotted down.

Drafting
Grammar and punctuation take a back seat to getting the ideas in place while a writer is drafting.

Revising
While revising, the author can elaborate, condense, or reorganize his or her draft. Sometimes the project takes an entirely new direction during this stage.

Editing
The wise writer knows that editing means paying careful attention to punctuation, spelling, grammar, transitions, and flow.

Publish and Share
Publishing can be as easy as getting the writing in final form for sharing. Put it in a folder, add an illustration, and make sure that it looks polished. Now it is ready to be shared with friends and family!

One last thought...
Show appreciation for good writing by pointing out examples of good writing that you encounter.

Synonyms
for Said

Your fourth grader is exploring his or her writing skills. Help him or her by balancing dialogue verbs between the word *said* and its synonyms.

admitted	begged	concluded
agreed	blurted	cried
answered	boasted	declared
argued	bragged	demanded
asked	bugged	described
	called	divulged
	chatted	exclaimed
	complained	explained

gasped	objected	stated
groaned	offered	taunted
grumbled	replied	teased
laughed	responded	wailed
lied	retorted	whimpered
mumbled	screamed	whined
murmured	shouted	whispered
muttered	sobbed	worried

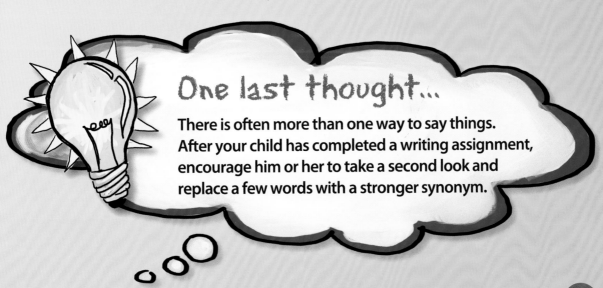

One last thought...

There is often more than one way to say things.
After your child has completed a writing assignment,
encourage him or her to take a second look and
replace a few words with a stronger synonym.

Math
Skills

Tackle problems with good humor, even if math is tough for you. Stay relaxed and be ready to break up math homework so that it isn't frustrating.

Try these tips to improve your child's math skills.

Try It Backwards

Teach how to check an answer by working the problem backwards. If it's a subtraction problem, check it by adding.

Be Strategic

If a problem seems difficult, break it into smaller steps. Make drawings or use manipulatives such as toothpicks or marbles.

Step by Step

1. Read it aloud two or three times, slowly.

2. Substitute big numbers with smaller numbers.

3. Draw a picture or diagram.

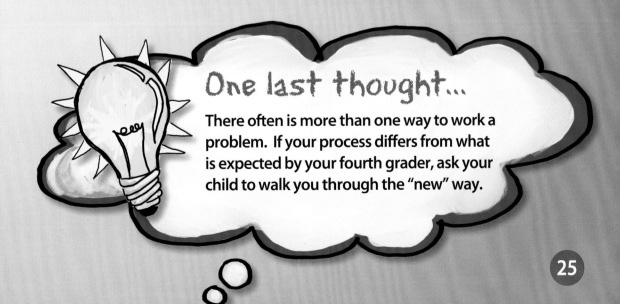

One last thought...

There often is more than one way to work a problem. If your process differs from what is expected by your fourth grader, ask your child to walk you through the "new" way.

Everyday
Math

Your fourth grader will be working hard on multiplication, long division, and fractions this year. Your kitchen is the perfect place to reinforce these math concepts—and to get some help, too!

Here are some fun ideas
to bring math into everyday activities.

Kitchen Math

Involve your child in doubling or tripling the ingredients for a recipe. This is a great time to teach how to add fractions.

Baking Problems

"We need to make 36 muffins for the bake sale. Each recipe makes a dozen muffins. How many batches do we need to make?"

Equipment Size

Getting the equipment right is just as important as accurately measuring the ingredients of a recipe. Let your child help you find everything you need for your cooking project.

"Read the recipe and find out what size pan we need."

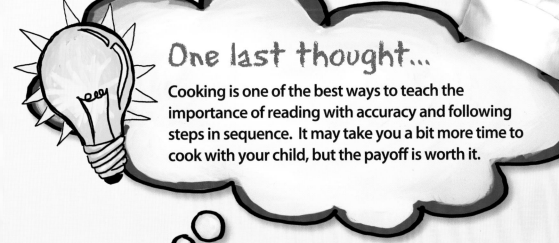

One last thought...

Cooking is one of the best ways to teach the importance of reading with accuracy and following steps in sequence. It may take you a bit more time to cook with your child, but the payoff is worth it.

How to Do
Long Division

Fourth graders are learning more complex math skills. Review these tips to help improve your child's long division skills.

Change the way the problem is written.

$$3$$
$$2 \overline{)68}$$ $$6 ÷ 2 = 3$$

$$3$$
$$2 \overline{)68}$$ $$3 × 2 = 6$$
$$6$$

$$3$$ $$3$$
$$2 \overline{)68}$$ → $$2 \overline{)68}$$
$$- 6$$ $$- 6↓$$
$$0$$ $$08$$

$$34$$
$$2 \overline{)68}$$ $$8 ÷ 2 = 4$$
$$- 6$$
$$08$$

$$34$$ Check:
$$2 \overline{)68}$$ $$34 × 2 = 68$$
$$- 6$$
$$08$$
$$- 8$$

Science
All Around

Your fourth grader is exploring life, earth, and physical science.
Help foster his or her learning about investigations with food,
life forms, and plants and animals and their environments.

These activities will help your child to think critically about science.

Cause and Effect

Simple cause-and-effect experiments can be set up with inexpensive plants. Vary the watering, fertilizing, and lighting. Make predictions about how these changes might affect the plant.

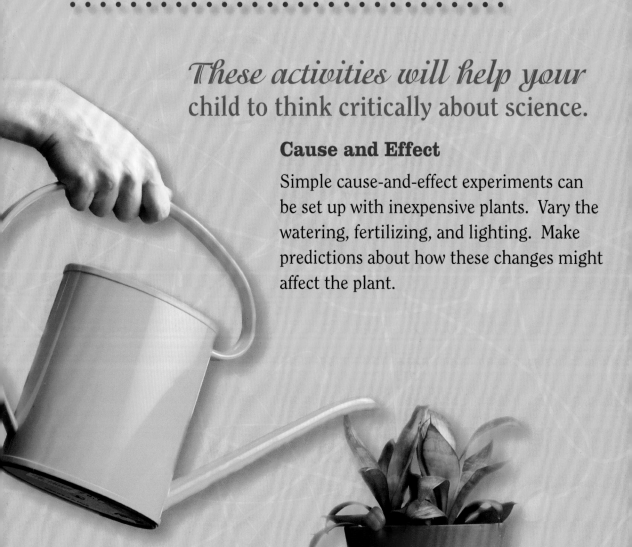

Food Science

Try to figure out why raisins dropped into a carbonated drink "dance" after a few minutes. Soak an egg or chicken bone in vinegar and see what happens in a couple of days.

Earth Science

A deeper understanding of the relationship between life forms and Earth (and sky) is fostered this year. Don't hold back—become an investigator along with your youngster!

Human Body

A trip to the doctor's office is a good time to learn about the human body. Encourage lots of questions.

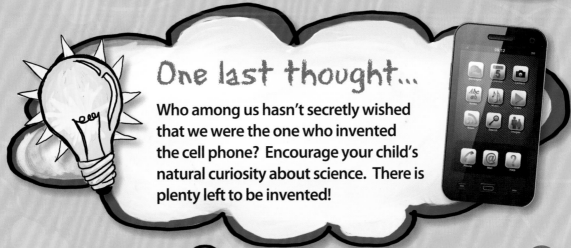

One last thought...

Who among us hasn't secretly wished that we were the one who invented the cell phone? Encourage your child's natural curiosity about science. There is plenty left to be invented!

Social Studies
Skills

Your fourth grader is learning about key events in your state's history and the national government.

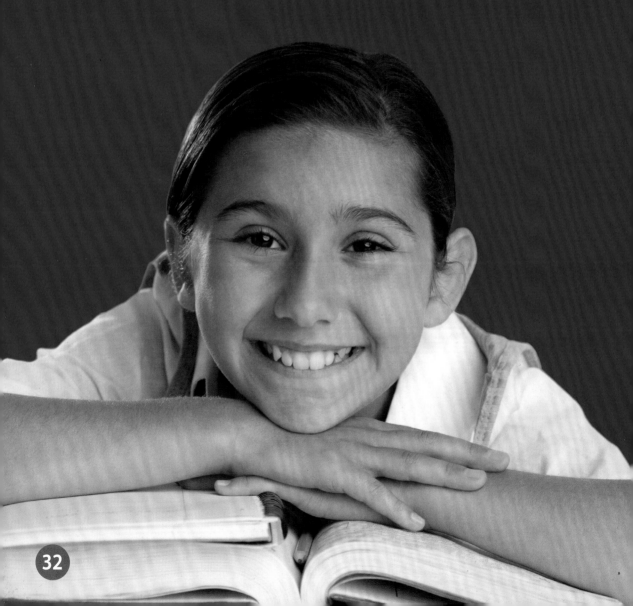

Help your child develop an awareness of history and diversity with these activities.

Use a Map

Use a program such as Google Maps to look up your home address. From the bird's-eye view, expand to see what your neighborhood and city look like from above.

Around the World

Compare your community to those of relatives around the world.

Daily Newspaper

Subscribe to a daily newspaper for ongoing current events and history lessons.

Weather Page

Use the weather page to trace the effects of events such as a drought or a blizzard on people and the economy.

One last thought...

Celebrate your family history by capturing stories from the elders in your family. Ask your child's grandparents to write down or record favorite recipes, stories, and memories.

After-School
Balancing Act

It's important to strike a balance so that there is plenty of time for your child to decompress. Enroll him or her in an after-school program so your child can take a break from school and studying and enjoy extracurricular activities.

Sciences

Check your local science museum for classes on chemistry experiments.

Sports

Your city league has lots of different sports for your young child. Discuss with your child beforehand about which team he or she would like to join.

Arts

The arts center in your neighborhood may be offering community classes on making videos, painting, or dance.

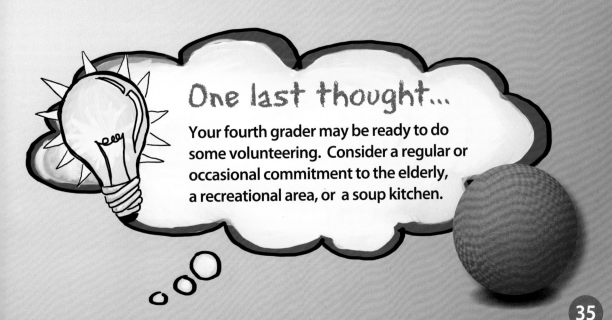

One last thought...

Your fourth grader may be ready to do some volunteering. Consider a regular or occasional commitment to the elderly, a recreational area, or a soup kitchen.

On the Road
Again

Turn your everyday trips in the community and beyond into rich learning experiences using these recommendations. Everyone will be more involved, and you may not hear "Are we there yet?" anymore!

Tour Guide

Before taking a trip, turn your child into a trip organizer. Contact the chamber of commerce or use the Internet to investigate places to visit during the trip. Let your fourth grader actively plan the trip by being the tour guide.

Photographer

Invest in a digital camera to record both local and longer trips. For local trips, have your child take thematic pictures, capturing varied themes: cows, laundry on the line, birds, chairs on porches, mailboxes, billboards, etc. For longer trips, have your fourth grader combine photography with a journal of the trip.

One last thought...

Put together a travel bag or backpack that holds a variety of materials, such as word puzzles, a clipboard, paper, and pencils.

Family
Fun

Fourth grade isn't all about studying and work. Your child still loves to play, and research tells us that play is always important. Through group games, we learn to think strategically, solve problems, and even get some exercise.

Try some of these ideas to bring fun into your family!

Races and Relays

Place oversized clothes in two bags. Each player on the team runs up, puts on the clothes, removes the clothes, and then runs back. Or, put all your shoes in a pile. Each player runs up, finds his or her shoes, puts them on, and runs back.

Theme Garden

Create a theme garden, such as a salsa, butterfly, alphabet (a plant for every letter), or bee garden. No yard? You can grow a lot of plants in pots or find a community garden.

Board Games

Don't forget how fun board games can be! Board games are a great way to bring the family together for a little extra fun. If you want to try something new, have your fourth grader create a game for the whole family to play. Don't forget to have the rules written down!

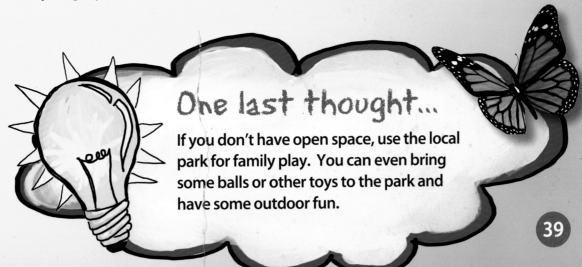

One last thought...

If you don't have open space, use the local park for family play. You can even bring some balls or other toys to the park and have some outdoor fun.

Dear Parent,

Your fourth grader is well on his or her way to becoming independent in many ways. This year is important for sustaining the close relationship you've built up during your child's lifetime. Keep the conversation going, make projects together, and have some fun. You may even find yourself relearning some old skills—and probably learning a few new ones!

We hope this parent guide has given you some good ideas to try out along the journey. Don't forget that the Internet is a good source for more ideas. Enjoy it all because in what seems like a minute, you'll have a fifth grader!

Thank you!